My First NFL Book

ARIZONA CARDINALS

Katie Gillespie

LET'S READ

AV² BY WEIGL™

ADDED VALUE • AUDIO VISUAL

Go to **www.av2books.com**, and enter this book's unique code.

BOOK CODE

R884548

AV² by Weigl brings you media enhanced books that support active learning.

AV² provides enriched content that supplements and complements this book. Weigl's AV² books strive to create inspired learning and engage young minds in a total learning experience.

Your AV² Media Enhanced books come alive with...

Audio
Listen to sections of the book read aloud.

Video
Watch informative video clips.

Embedded Weblinks
Gain additional information for research.

Try This!
Complete activities and hands-on experiments.

Key Words
Study vocabulary, and complete a matching word activity.

Quizzes
Test your knowledge.

Slide Show
View images and captions, and prepare a presentation.

... and much, much more!

Published by AV² by Weigl
350 5th Avenue, 59th Floor
New York, NY 10118

Website: www.av2books.com

Printed in the United States of America in Brainerd, Minnesota
1 2 3 4 5 6 7 8 9 0   21 20 19 18 17

032017
020317

Editor: Katie Gillespie
Art Director: Terry Paulhus

Weigl acknowledges Getty Images and Alamy as the primary image suppliers for this title.

Library of Congress Control Number: 2017930529

ISBN 978-1-4896-5478-6 (hardcover)
ISBN 978-1-4896-5480-9 (multi-user eBook)

My First NFL Book

ARIZONA CARDINALS

CONTENTS

3

Team History

The Cardinals first played football in 1898. The team started in Chicago, Illinois. They moved to Arizona almost 90 years later. This makes the Cardinals the oldest team in the NFL today.

Charley Trippi joined the Cardinals in 1945 as the NFL's #1 draft pick.

5

The Stadium

University of Phoenix Stadium is home to the Cardinals. The football field is made of natural grass. This grass is moved into the stadium before each game.

University of Phoenix Stadium is in Glendale, Arizona.

Team Spirit

Big Red is the team's mascot. His job is to cheer on the players. Big Red also helps to get the crowd excited. In his spare time, Big Red likes to visit children in local schools and hospitals.

Big Red likes to throw t-shirts to Cardinals fans.

The Jerseys

The first Cardinals jerseys were cardinal red. The team is named after this color. Today, the players wear three different jerseys. Their main colors are red, white, and black.

The Helmet

The Cardinals wear white helmets made of strong plastic. Every helmet has a cardinal-head logo on the side. Each player's number is on the back of his helmet.

In 1943, the NFL made it a rule for players to wear helmets.

13

The Coach

Bruce Arians is the head coach of the Cardinals. He led the team to 43 wins in his first 60 games. Arians was only the 11th person in history to win more than one NFL Coach of the Year award. His second win was in 2014 for coaching the Cardinals.

Player Positions

The offense includes the quarterback. He leads the team and runs the play. The defensive line includes the defensive ends. It is their job to stop the play from moving outside.

Special teams include the punter and the field goal kicker.

Larry Fitzgerald is one of the top Cardinals players. He has played wide receiver for the team since 2004. Fitzgerald was the youngest player ever to make 100 catches in a single season. Today, he is ranked #3 in all-time career receptions.

18

Kurt Warner played quarterback for the Cardinals from 2005 to 2009. He helped lead the team to its first Super Bowl in 2008. Warner threw for 377 yards during the game. This set a Super Bowl record as the second-highest total in history.

Team Records

The Cardinals have had many talented members over the years. Ken Whisenhunt led the team to a record 45 wins, the highest of any Cardinals coach. Jim Bakken was the team's all-time scoring leader, with a record 1,380 points. The Cardinals have appeared in 16 playoffs to date, including Super Bowl 2009.

Ken Whisenhunt
45 Wins

16 Playoff Appearances

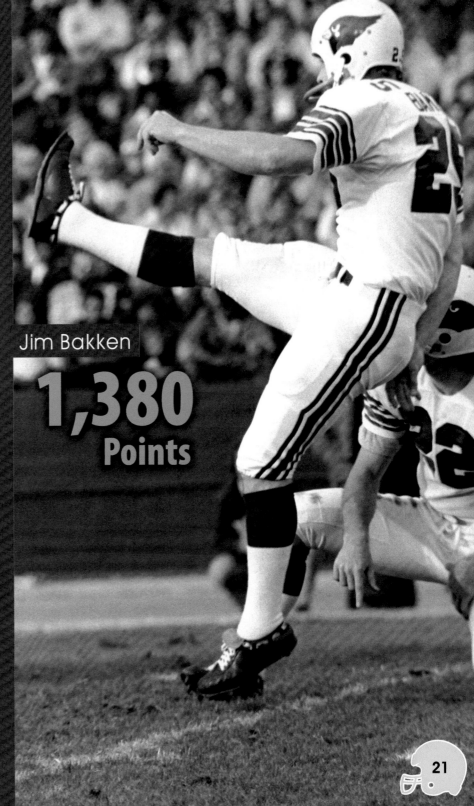

Jim Bakken
1,380 Points

21

By the Numbers

Big Red's wingspan is **7 feet** wide.

University of Phoenix Stadium opened in **2006.**

UNIVERSITY OF PHOENIX STADIUM

The Cardinals scored **489** points in **2015,** setting a team record for most points scored in a season.

The team had **6 other names** before becoming the **Arizona Cardinals.**

The largest home game in the Cardinals' history was attended by **73,025** fans.

The team's record for **most consecutive victories is 11.**

16 former Cardinals have been honored in the Pro Football Hall of Fame.

Quiz

1. What is the team named after?

2. Who is the current head coach of the Cardinals?

3. In which year did the Cardinals first play football?

4. How many former Cardinals have been honored in the Pro Football Hall of Fame?

5. In what position is Larry Fitzgerald ranked for all-time career receptions?

Check out www.av2books.com for activities, videos, audio clips, and more!

1 Go to www.av2books.com.

2 Enter book code. | R 8 8 4 5 4 8 |

3 Fuel your imagination online!

www.av2books.com